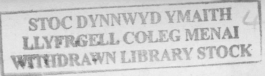

Bed

Bed was premièred at the National Theatre in the Cottesloe on 8 March 1989.

'Future historians of absurdist theatre will surely have to take note of Jim Cartwright and *Bed*, an elegiac dream-and-memory play as fascinatingly weird as anything penned by Samuel Beckett, the dean of absurdity himself.'   *Variety*

'The writing is, in Cartwright's unique way, both spartan and rococo; as a script the structure of the piece is frighteningly destructured, encompassing surreal word-games, dark narratives reminiscent of *Road*. . .'
                    Alex Renton, *The Independent*

'Cartwright's ear for language is as acute as ever and *Bed* is studded with affection, nostalgia and real human emotions.'
                    Peter Wilson, *Times Literary Supplement*

'There is more here than just mellow pillow-talk. The disconnected arias of old age find a new form . . . the heartbeat of an entire existence is caught in a series of interlinked memories.'
                    Michael Coveney, *The Financial Times*

Jim Cartwright is the author of the play **Road** of which Alex Renton wrote in *The Independent:* 'perhaps the most inspiring and exciting state-of-the-nation piece that the Eighties have seen.' In 1986 **Road** scooped the Samuel Beckett Award, *Drama* Magazine award and was joint winner of the George Devine Award and the Plays and Players Award. A version for television won the Golden Nymph Award for the best film at the Monte Carlo Festival.

by the same author

**Road
To**

Jim Cartwright

Bed

METHUEN DRAMA

A Methuen Modern Play

First published in Great Britain as a paperback original in
1991 by Methuen Drama, Michelin House, 81 Fulham Road,
London SW3 6RB and distributed in the United States of
America by HEB Inc., 361 Hanover Street, Portsmouth,
New Hampshire 03801.
Revised and reprinted in 1991.

Copyright © 1991 by Jim Cartwright

A CIP catalogue record for this book is available from The
British Library.

Photograph of the author on the back cover is © Mark
Gerson. Front cover photograph is from the original 1989
National Theatre production. © Simon Annand.

ISBN 0–413–62230–4

Printed and bound by Cox & Wyman Ltd, Reading

Caution

Bed was first performed at the National Theatre on 8 March 1989 with the following cast:

Captain	John Boswell
Charles	Charles Simon
Sermon Head	Graham Crowden
The Couple	Donald Bisset and Joan White
Marjorie	Margery Withers
Spinster	Vivienne Burgess
Bosom Lady	Ruth Kettlewell

Director	Julia Bardsley
Designer	Peter J. Davison
Lighting	Christopher Toulmin
Music	John Winfield

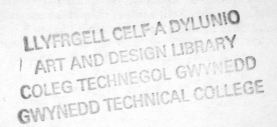

In the half light we see a bedroom with a big bed, 30ft wide or more, almost covering the stage. Up one side of the room a mountain of armchairs and a massive window and curtains. Up the other side a chest of drawers mountain and, high on the wall, a little wooden cabinet upside down.

Directly over the bed is a shelf, on which are many bedtime things covered in dust: books, bottle and spoon, broken alarm clock etc. and a thing which looks like a head or bust but is not too clear in the half dark.

We hear breathing.

Lights come up further and we are aware of seven elderly people lying in bed.

Bosom Lady I'm too warm.

Captain I'm boiling.

Charles I'm boiled.

Spinster We've all got our aches and pains.

Marjorie On the edge of sleep.

Bosom Lady Toffee eyes.

Captain I love sleeping but I can never get deep like the old days.

The Couple We share it.

Charles I suck on sleep like a boiled sweet.

Spinster Speaking of boiled, I am.

Marjorie Moon-calf. Moon-calf.

Bosom Lady Asleep in the ooze.

Bosom Lady *pulls a biscuit out of her cleavage, nibbles it.*

Charles Pass the biscuit.

Spinster Gum the crumbs.

Marjorie Mattress of bread.

Bosom Lady Well, we're all toasting it then.

Captain Speak up, I can't hear over here.

Charles No one's 'spose to, it's sleep time.

Spinster I wish I could. I wish I could. Not even a pill can help.

Marjorie Count sheep.

Captain Count sheep's arses.

Bosom Lady You old toothless dirty mouth.

Charles Shave sheep and sleep in the wool coils.

Spinster I could 'cause I always knit sleep round me.

Marjorie It is a slow thing coming I'll grant you.

Bosom Lady It takes its time.

The Couple We save sleep up.

Charles When I close my eyes, where am I? When I open them, where?

Spinster When I close my eyes, all sorts drop. When I open them after that the dark's all in pieces.

Marjorie It's like black sand when it shifts.

Bosom Lady Heavy on your chest.

Captain Pressing your breaths.

Charles I'm telepathic.

Spinster The mattress has me now.

Charles I know.

Bosom Lady Give up the ghost.

Captain (*looking under the blankets*) When you think how underwear's changed through the ages.

Charles God I wish I was under the sea, a sea sleep.

Spinster Sea-rious.

Marjorie He certainly is.

Bosom Lady My dreams are silent movies.

Captain Give us the snore song someone.

Charles I dream westerns.

The Couple We dream in time.

Spinster Who are we, where do we go?

Marjorie Cuddle me. Cuddle me.

Captain Are there refreshments.

Charles Shall we pray.

Bosom Lady (*beginning to drift off again*) Dreaming again. Folding and unfolding white again.

Charles (*going also*) A shower of feathers and snow.

Spinster (*brushes mattress as she goes*) Sugar in the bed.

They are all beginning to fall.

Bosom Lady We all lie back and just whisp away.

Back to sleep.

Long pause.

Charles *suddenly sits bolt upright.*

Charles I'm off. I put my driving hat on. (*Takes trilby out from under sheets, puts it on.*) Turn the key. Over the kerb. Nice sound underneath. Round the village pond. (*Leans into it as he goes. Waves to someone.*) Hello. Steady now over the bumps and holes. Bloody things! (*Sees someone.*) Morning Vicar. Yes splendid. Oh dear. (*Changes gear.*) Up the wee brew. Come on you can do it girl. Stop at the top.

Bosom Lady *suddenly comes up beside him with a basket on her arm.*

Bosom Lady Hello.

Charles (*surprised*) Oh.

Bosom Lady Could you just stop at the bottom shop so I can buy some strawberry jam again.

Charles Okay. But hold on tight. (*Lets brake go.*) Because here we go!

They shoot down the hill.

Bosom Lady Whoooooooooooooooooooooooo.

Charles Ha harrrrrrrrrr.

They stop at the bottom.

Bosom Lady Won't be a mo.

Charles I'll leave the engine running.

She's gone under the covers.

Captain Psss.

Charles *looks round.*

Captain It's me old boy. Going far?

Charles Could be, not sure yet.

Captain Mind if I join you?

Charles I er . . . . . .

Captain (*clinks bottles under the blankets*) I've a few fresh stout here. (*Clinks again.*)

Charles (*friendly*) Clamber in old chap, there's a rug at the back, slip them under.

He lifts **Charles**' *pillow to slip them behind.*

Captain What's this, white chicken and ham. A beautiful cheese. An apple pie.

Charles Shush. Sh. Sh.

Suddenly everyone's up and sniffing in their sleep, following their noses.

Bosom Lady (*comes back with shopping*) Strawberries, chocolate cake, spam.

At this **Marjorie** *and* **Spinster** *and* **The Couple** *clamber in on each side behind* **Charles**. **The Couple** *though sitting up remain asleep. In front,* **Captain** *is one side of* **Charles**, **Bosom Lady** *the other.*

Spinster } Are we off then?
Marjorie }

Charles (*with a car full, giving in*) Oh werry vell. Werry vell.

Captain Come on the anchors away!

Spinster }
Marjorie } Yes yes.
Bosom Lady }

Marjorie Foot well down. (**Charles** *presses his horn.*) PEEP PEEP!

Spinster Wheels free.

They all shudder forward.

Marjorie We're off!

They move as though travelling. All happy.

Charles The tickle belly bridge.

They bump over it.

All Wooooooooooooooo. (*Laughter.*)

Charles Down the tree lined.

They all press forward.

And out, out into the open road.

Spinster (*leans over*) Not so fast Charles. Faster!

She giggles.

Bosom Lady Yes race him. (*A passing car.*) Oh he's gone.

Charles Has he.

He suddenly changes gear. They all make the sound of the car as they surge forward. Wind blasted. Racing. They pass the other car. They all cheer. Wave. Pull faces. Blow raspberries. Blow kisses. As they pass.

Charles (*proud*) Here we go!

At the back they begin sharing out the food and beer.

– Anyone like a

– Lovely.

– Anyone like a

– Lovely.

– Anyone.

– Lovely.

– Anyone like a.

Charles Don't forget your driver.

Bosom Lady Here we go. Chicken leg one side.

He takes a bite, as she holds it.

Marjorie Beer the other. (*She pours some in his mouth.*)

They drive and eat.

Charles Look at that. Trees and then the lake. Trees and then the lake and the sun sliced on it.

Bosom Lady Oh I love this way round.

Marjorie The sun's making the road sparkle.

Spinster You feel as though you can catch things as you pass.

Bosom Lady *makes to catch something.*

Spinster What's that?

Bosom Lady A leaf.

Marjorie *catches something.*

Spinster What's that?

Marjorie A little bird. (*Lets it go.*) There she goes.

The women all blow a kiss.

Captain *catches something.*

Spinster What's that?

Captain Some litter. (*Undoes the crumpled paper a bit.*) No a poem. England . . .

Charles *begins to say it. As he does, they all settle back down to sleep.* **Captain** *with the paper over his face.* **Charles** *continues out.*

Charles England you summer beast. You humped bridges, you singing streams, you bumble hum, you round the cottage door. England you waxy rose. You scent. You hay stem in the mouth. You peasant-backed, rich-fronted, meadows and cheese and slow turn place. England you bowler hat/crown. You English Englishness English England. You green thing. You shape. You British school of motoring. You decent breakfast. You lived in land. You and your deep green indented green covered parts. Your cities sprung and crooked and sooted and historical. Stone England. Lassie and Laddie and Lord Land. You're pinched up in places and flattened in others, you have pubs and crannies and nooks, woods and brooks, fag end and piss precincts and towns of seventies cement, and modern, the word modern. And little birds lost and coughing. And motorways strapped across the fat of your land. Dark black, lit yellow. Cars come under the lights and the bridges and inside the automobiles people's heads are buzzing, they are. There's noises that have built up over the past thirty years, new and not right and in front and behind, and the brains gone puff ball, or modernly cooked, micro chumped. Beamed. Sucky. Not to be held. Past the sell-by date. Modern man has always just eaten. He's yellowed and flabby ripe. He's useless, killable. Standing in his underpants in the middle of the motorway with a personal hi-fi on.

Charles }
Captain } Screaming his bloody balls off.

Charles There's no more room in England any more for a Tra lu lu lal lal lah.

Captain *lets the paper go out the window.*

Bosom Lady I sometimes think that, and I think what a hard day's night.

They all sing the Beatles' song 'A Hard Day's Night' as they drive.

Charles Life on the open road.

Marjorie Where we going this night?

They all freeze. The lights go.

Charles You shouldn't have said night, it's gone dark now.

Bosom Lady Oh it's pitch black.

Charles Hang on. (*Makes a cluck sound with his mouth. Two of them turn on little torches under the sheet and hold them one each side as headlights.*)

They begin to travel again slowly. Slowly.

Spinster Don't go too fast down here Charles.

Bosom Lady What's that noise?

Marjorie Are there ghosts?

Captain Don't ask me, ask outside.

Bosom Lady (*looking out*) The leaves have gone black leather.

Spinster Wet too.

Marjorie It'll rain next.

Charles Watch what you say. Watch what you say.

Spinster Where are we?

Charles Is there no map?

Bosom Lady No.

Captain Yes. (*He lets the sheet crumple across his lap like a relief map and follows the folds and contours with his finger.*)

Charles We're just passing some black tucked in and shining.

Captain (*following map*) Yes yes.

Bosom Lady And a hazy dark a bit shut.

Captain (*still following the signs*) Yes yes.

Marjorie And some tall night tight, no swollen.

Captain Yes yes.

Spinster Then a corner offered. Then taken back.

Captain Yes yes.

Bosom Lady Some flittery shade.

Captain Right then! Just take the next, and there it is, a bright house of refreshment.

Marjorie Not ghosts?

Captain Not according to this.

She kisses him.

They all lean as though taking a big corner.

Charles And here we are.

To the left of them appears an area of bright light.

They go a little apprehensive again as **Charles** *stands up and walks slowly over the bed and looks into the space of light, then turns back towards them.*

Charles It's a damn disco. Come on in.

They all cross the bed and into the light, happy. They cram into the space of light. It's pleasant. They are dancing, dancing. Lights dim on them. Suddenly the head on the shelf opens its mouth and speaks.

Sermon Head
Here I am!
I'm here!
The constantly awake,
never slept,
shelved but
ever seeing,
spying my chances
with my raw eye (*Opens it wider, burning red.*)
and his partner 'Eaten'. (*Opens other, the same.*)
To cock up your kip.
All I've got, my
eyes, mouth, spittle,
skin, all of me, 'Why not take all of me'

You wouldn't would you? Would you.
You have to.
All of me
sheds out irritation
by the night-cap full
I shed irritation all through
till dawn
and I shed it with glee
with night-twisting glee.
I savour any wakings I can cause in them.
I savour every one.
They're all that keep me
going in here, in this 'all-I've-got head'. (*Eyes shut, shaking his head about, as though trying to get out of it.*)
Head! Head! Head!
Sleep doesn't want me.
Did I tell you.
Arrrrrrrrrrrrrrrrrrrrrrrrrrrrrrrrrhhh !
(*Half shouted, sung, at top pitch.*)
UH CHU CHU CHEE!
UH CHEE CHU CHEE CHU CHU!
UH CHU CHU CHEE!
UH CHEE CHU CHEE CHU CHU!
UH CHU CHU CHEE . . .

This disturbs the dancers. Lights dim on him and up on dancers, who are very disturbed now by the noise. They dance on but uncomfortable now. The disco seems crowded. The atmosphere has become unpleasant. They get nasty with each other. They argue bunched tightly together moving across the bed, still in the space of light and its boundaries, moving, the light going with them.

Sermon Head *stops singing, his purpose accomplished. They break and all return to bed, sitting up in bed now in a glum row. (Except* **The Couple** *who have gone to sleep.) Still angry with each other.*

Throughout the following speech, they begin to doze off again.

Sermon Head As you can imagine I've made a life long study of sleep. I've become what you might call obsessional and snoozle fanatical. But 'tis pure academical and leaves me still distanced from that one article, of my desire, sleep. Oh sleep, sleep sweet roller, kiss the inside of

Sermon Head's lids and let me fall into thee. (*Closes his eyes. Opens them.*) Why not, eh? WHERE IS MY SHARE? Oh stop it Sermon Head grab yourself together. Hold your head up. Look the night right in the eye. (*He does, his eyes wide open, burning raw red.*) Look with these raging balls and sawn off sockets. Open. There. Bam. Bam.

Suddenly from sleep all of them.

All Shut up Sermon Head!

Sermon Head Oh now we have it. Here they come as usual. Sympathy, whatever happened to it? They're at me again. Taunters. Mattress yobs.

They shout. Throw things at him.

Charles Pipe down!

Sermon Head I can't wear pyjamas!

Spinster Close it!

Couple Sssssssssssh.

Sermon Head I've never stretched!

Marjorie Oh stop.

Captain Shut the trap.

Charles Quit while you're a head.

They all laugh.

Sermon Head Oh very funny.

Spinster (*mocking*) He can't ever sleep.

Sermon Head I can so. I'm just on a sleep diet that's all.

They laugh.

Sleep fats!

They ignore him.

I'll get you lot and I bloody well will. Oh yes snore on. Snore on. . . . . .

They all settle back to sleep.

I'll have a go at them. I hate them. They keep their sleep in the bank. Full vaults or overdrawn up the nostrils. Well I want 'em wakened. I wish there were more ways available to me. Wish I was a Thermostat Face, red cheek gauged. Then I could chill or could concentrate up a heat, could bake their little throats. Look at those throats all in a row like beige sausage. Like sausage rolls. Crisp up throats, crack and buckle, flake. (*He blows dust from off the shelf onto them.*)

Marjorie *gives a cough.*

Got one anyway.

Marjorie (*waking*) So thirsty oh I'm dry.

No reply.

Oh I can't sleep for it.

Captain Don't worry there. Get your head under the ocean like me.

Marjorie I'll try. So sorry all.

Spinster What is it?

Bosom Lady Her little throat keeps telling her.

Charles Halt the breath between your lips. Sip it right down then start again.

Bosom Lady Is that what you do. You genius.

Marjorie Oh so thirsty.

Bosom Lady Use your spit dear.

Sermon Head *laughs.*

Spinster Think of water.

Captain Yes sink of water.

Couple Don't mention the stuff. It makes it worse.

Charles Clunk your tongue round, there might be some juice left.

Sermon Head *laughs.*

Bosom Lady Water! Water! Water to do!

Captain I'm tucking in the waves all round, nice and cosy and splashy.

Marjorie So thirsty it's hurting.

Spinster Sssssssh you're starting me off now.

Couple Sufferings sufferings.

Sermon Head Belt up and bring her a glass of water for sleepssake!

Silence. They are all still but with eyes wide open, tense. Pause.

Couple (*slowly*) We'll go for the glass of water.

Marjorie Thank you so very much. How can I ever . . .

All of them begin pulling back the blankets and sheets industriously, busy doing their different tasks like a trained crew. The blankets are rolled back. Pillows mounted. Covers untucked. Sheets tied and knotted etc. **The Couple** *during this are putting on their dressing-gowns and slippers. The others proceed to the bed centre on all fours or knees, and ease up and ease out and ease up then suddenly out a perfect round shape of mattress, a clear lid. The slices of sheet and spring are very visible at the side like a piece of cake. And as it leaves the hole a beam of light shoots right up strong to the ceiling. They then proceed to lower* **The Couple** *down the hole by the knotted sheets. When they are out of sight they solemnly close the lid, restore the sheets etc. and silently return to bed. Then to sleep.*

Sermon Head I'm still awake. I have to mention it. You see how I had them, worried, well wakened. Staring into the light, like me. And now they're right back where we started. Sleep's too magnetic in its drawing. Won't drag me off into its dark suck though will it. Oh, you leave me so jealous! You sleep easies – You yawn friends. Slumber dogs. Doing your greed sleeping. Snoring. Lip fluttering under the covers and blankets, wool and cotton all over your mouths. Breath swopping. Look at you all in your dream wigs.

They wake.

Bosom Lady Shut up Sermon Head.

Captain Get slept.

Sermon Head Look at you in that lovely big bed, you're not worthy of it. When I think of the bed my poor Mother headed. A dirty bed. A 'kicked' bed. Squeaking in its hundred voices, the stinking square. Always moving. A corner torn off. Full of old hands and the soft sinky breasts of Victorian chars . . .

Charles Shut him up, someone.

Spinster Give him the poke.

One of them quickly pulls from under the bed a very long duster, (as long as it needs to be to reach him) sharp end first, and using this end pokes him right in the cheek with it. He starts squealing at top pitch. They poke him again. He shuts up. The duster is returned. They turn over and sleep.

Blackout.

Lights up on **The Couple**, *who are half-way up and still scaling the armchair mountain. They stop and rest in a couple of the chairs.*

Woman To

Man gether.

Woman Tied.

They kick off and the armchairs suddenly swing out and very gently go back and forth out over the bed like swings.

Woman Shared.

Man We've shared ourselves away to each other.

Woman I'd give you my air and you'd return it with yours.

Man Do we still love we.

Woman It is love but we're making it last. Are we happy?

Man I've forgotten. Did you put the cat out?

Woman Twenty years ago.

Man And it never came back the swine.

Both
One hand, one wrist, one arm. Our minds
have faded together.
Our souls are hugging.
There's only a second betwixt our hearts beats
enough just for separation.
They go
  we're two no one
    two one
  we're two no one
    two one.

Both (*sing*)
We are the kinder things of life
We place our breaths
We're in the air almost

Man We're done in watercolours.

Woman Our hearts go like rocking chairs.

Sermon Head What about the glass of water, you stupid old
sods!

They remember, park up the armchairs and hurry away.

He turns his attention to those below, still smarting from poke.

(*Whispering.*) I'll give you all sore pillows, sore pillows I will.
I'll make that a sick bed I will, I'll . . .

Someone turns over below. He goes quiet.

(*Looking at them all sleeping.*) You sod gums. You . . . Just
look at them. I hate that. They'll hate this. Well one will. (*He
starts to laugh. He gently and softly sings an old sea shanty.*)

This disturbs **Captain.** *He begins tossing and turning, thrashing
the bed-clothes. Pulling them off the others. They all pull them back.
He pulls them off. They pull them back.*

Captain (*in sleep*) No. Hold. Don't falter. Lash. Criss cross.
Send it back overboard, fill your palms with the salty stuff
and throw. Sea leave me!

He seems to settle again. Then **Sermon Head** *very softly and low* *sings a little more of the sea shanty. (Throughout this speech a great storm builds, the window blows open and a powerful gale thrashes the curtains. The others huddle in their sleep.)*

Oh not again. You blaster. I've washed tonight, I've brushed my reef. Oh no here I go. I'm up. I'm down. Hold me someone. It's raging again. The storm. All my belongings are out on the deck, travelling, like swimming sheep following each other over the side, drank away. Skidding books, wet, slapped on the wood, gone. The rains bouncing feets high. I'm going to hold on. Oh yes I am. I'm going to hold. Trapped between two ragers, the sky and the sea, hopelessly caught in the zig-zag between. We're high then low. Bouncing. Sometimes suspended a second, in so much noise it's like silence. Then flung down again. Spun and slanted by the sea. It can't bear us on its surface. There's a dead dog on the deck, (*The ladies scream, then back to sleep.*) spinning around and around in the skud, then gone. I shall hold. Oh I shall hold. It's gathering now all of it and I'm in the mid. I'm waiting. I'm holding. I'm gripping on, arms around the mast. My legs sea-logged, thrown about. I've bitten my lip off, it came away like wet paper. I'm biting my bite now. Thoughts won't stay, my mind's slid. I'm cold, numb, slub. There's my will. I can see it before my eyes. A cannon barrel. Hold. Pray hold. And you and you and you. I wish you were here now. And she, where's gone, where's gone . . . Pray from right under. Pray deep under. Pray over. Pray over. Praysa! Praysa! (*Lets out an almighty cry.*) Grarrrrrrrrrrrrrrrrrrrrrrrrrrrrrrrrrrrrrrrrrrrrrrrrrrrrrrr! (*Suddenly, looking high and around, still standing, arms out, as though in the air. Startled, wonder-struck.*) Now I'm in a great and total circle of sea. Now thrown. But it's like flying. (*Goes down.*) Suddenly I'm in the water, supported. (*Lies down in stages.*) It's like a chair, now a plank, now wet cloth. Now my limbs are spread and free, sea-surrounded, it's hurrying to fit all my outside spaces, between my arms and body, between my legs. Warm salt waters. Lulled, passed from wave to wave. Then a seagull, the cliffs and headboard. I'm back washed up on the bed. Pillow-shored. Glad to be alive. Sea-gargled. Calm.

All their breaths and snoring become that of a calm sea off a shore.

The wind has died away. But the window is still open. **The Couple** *are perched on the window sill. Still shaken by the storm and clutching onto each other. They close the window.*

Woman (*afraid*) Oh dear.

Man Which way is it now?

Woman It's going on a long time. Are you shaking?

Man Yes I quite am.

Woman So am I.

Man I have to put your hair back it's all over the place.

He begins to do this.

Woman (*for comfort*) Bring your face close. Closer, I don't want to see it all in one go. But closer still. I want to read a little to comfort me. Our times together have turned the skin, made beautiful lines.

Man I'm still in your hair.

Woman Where did your face come from?

Man *shakes his head, still sorting her hair out.*

Woman (*she is silently going over his face, touches a mark on his skin*) Who put that there? (*Silence as she continues looking over face, closer.*) I go from one true story to another. In your smooth skin, shades, foldage and lines, I see the all of us. I . . . Closer. Close. Closer still. (*They grip tightly in an embrace.*)

Light fades off them and up on **Sermon Head.**

Sermon Head (*glares down at the sleepers*) Zedding hogs. Sleep sippers and spitters. Look at 'em cooking in their own snoring heat. One nose after another. Oh but really and truly what could be better than a night in bed. You cannot get a good English sleep these days. I can't even get a takeaway. They're not worthy of sleep them snore hogs. I am. So am. Number one sleep fan, student, swot. I've grasped all its degrees, I've got Forty Winks after me name. I've classified every type. One's sleep is well used. Another second hand. One's is brittle. One's is see-through. One's is alchemical. One's is passed around. One's a sleepskin rug. One's ladling sleep from a bucket. One has the bonfire smell. One's is bread hot. One's is very wrong. One's is clot. One's is like hands in beautiful hair. There's all these sleep sorts and more, oh yes more. But none come near Sermon Head, I can't even get a thin thread of it. It's just not me. Doesn't go with my eyes.

Stops. Then starts forming crossword words.

One down
Two, two across
Four down
Three.

Charles (*in sleep*) Three up.

Captain (*in sleep*) Two across.

Marjorie (*in sleep*) One down.

Captain How many letters?

Charles *awakes, gets his newspaper and pen out. Sits up. Starts doing the crossword.*

Spinster (*in sleep*) Yes I'm feeling better.

Bosom Lady (*in sleep*) Are you?

Captain Two was it two?

Charles No it was five.

Marjorie Is there a 'C'?

Captain I've just been in the sea.

Bosom Lady Was it five?

Captain No, one in it?

Marjorie That's me, I'll knit. (*She awakes, gets her knitting, Sits up.*)

Bosom Lady Who' won it?

Captain Is there an 'I' in it?

Spinster I'll iron it. (*Sits up, still in sleep. Starts smoothing pillow*) I have to.

Charles No, there was an 'S' in it.

Bosom Lady S . . O . .

Captain I'll take four Gallions.

Charles He's back in the bloody sea.

Captain Aye aye.

Bosom Lady 'I' in it.

Spinster I am ironing it!

Bosom Lady Sure there was an 'O' in it.

Captain One or two 'O's in it. Toes in it. (*He awakes, sits up to clip his toes.*)

Charles 'C' . . .

Marjorie Who do you see?

Bosom Lady (*awakes, sitting up, looking in hand mirror*) Me.

Charles 'D' that's it
D.I.S.C.O.
Disco!

He fills it in.

Spinster *awakes, stands indicating the mess the bed is in after the storm.*

Spinster
Ahhh this I can no longer abide.
Neither should they.
Chaos, a roughed den in which sin can hide.
With vigour my hands shake it out.
I rawl disorder.
And I can go a choking in the thrown about.

She grabs a pile of sheets and blankets as though throttling them, and throws them straight. She continues moving over the bed, restoring it.

Even in my birth I
nipped singularly all my
Mother's side
I came out clean, not covered in blood,

a matron slide.
Since then it has always been my way,
Scouring life.
Setting standards that never stray.
(*She suddenly strokes the darkness itself.*)
The night itself I like a good black.
As from old cross or kettle
Coated back
Edwardian metal
Not too lit upon.
Rubbed or seared
to the dark of my religion.

She tries to move the blankets from **Bosom Lady** *who won't let her.*
Spinster *punches her hard in her big arm.* **Bosom Lady** *howls.*
She hits her again on the exact same spot.

Charles	Hey steady on!
Marjorie	Leave her be!
Captain	Hey!

She spins to face them arms upraised in a terrifying gesture of kill.
Hands clasped over her head, holds it, shaking shaking with anger.
Bosom Lady *moves for her. Then she brings clasped hands over to*
a kind of praying position in front of her chest, then lets them go.
And continues tidying as though nothing had happened.

Spinster
Strangely I find that in place of love, hate
is often the best
cleaning agent
to penetrate and separate.
(*Continues her work.*)
My body has kept well. Kept out of sight.
My breast bared
to no babe or light (*She touches her breasts.*)
Two sheet corners sharpened
squeezed only by age
Milkless and whitened
Bit beaten with rage.

Sermon Head Shut up you old bag!

Spinster *reaches under bed, pulls out feather duster sharp end first.* **Sermon Head** *starts screaming. Then she turns it round to the big feathered side of the duster. He sighs with relief. She reaches up with it and briskly knocks him off the shelf. The head falls screaming to the bed. In his sleep* **Charles** *puts it under a pillow to quiet it.* **Spinster** *continues making bed.*

Spinster
This our country needs remaking
As I remake this
Its foundations are flaking
Its spirit misshapen
There's a smell rising
From where our tradition has been forsaken
It's under beds and off the shore
Putrification.
England hangs off the map
half scrounger, half whore.
Oh Britannia,
doing anything to get fat.
Morally sparse.
Fast-fingered heathens steal her crown
while mauling her arse.

She has almost finished off the tucking in. It is much too tight over them. Tucked in so tight they can hardly breathe.

As I turn back the covers
straight-lined
I also turn back my mind
to my memories, mainly
neatly stacked ashes. (*Her mood changes.*)
Save that one, the one
Where the wind over the moor dashes.
An almighty wind
Apostles in the grasses,
Cloistered trees unbound,
Sky and clod earth
shoving out the cathedral sound.
A young me there, thumping
with nature
Hymns all over my hair,
a Bible picture.

She stops herself and squeezes under tight sheets.

My life's a commandment
and in it I'm entrenched
My heart feels like a giant
silent choir clenched.
Wants to sing
after all these years,
But I've tightened it in
with ribs and fears.
Many other inner organs
are the same way gagged.
Bitterness runneth over
But love on the sharp ends
of my bigoted bones gets snagged.
(*Getting the line of the sheet under her chin just right.*)
You see I have to do my right
Keep account.
Perfect nib must be
lifted clean from page each night.
My life ledger *will be in order*
I shall not be shook off.
I have my teeth and
claws, in my God's cold shoulder.

She looks out. She looks up with just her eyes.

(*Under her breath, hard.*) Turn that light out.

Blackout.

The **Couple Man** *in a corner by himself, her slipper in his hand.
Lost.*

Man I am lost. We have got somehow separated. It's cold on
own. My breathing's gone all funny. There's dark
everywhere. (*He looks around.*) Is this loneliness? (*Pause.*)
How did I get here? I can't remember. She looked after the
memory. (*Pause.*) Was I dreaming her all these years? (*Looks
at slipper.*) Oh my dearest, I have your smell and fluff, but
you you.

Suddenly three little cries come, almost like a phone ringing. It is coming from the slipper. He puts it to his ear.

Hello.

*Lights come up on **Woman**. She has the other slipper at her ear. Talks into it.*

Woman Who is this please?

Man Is that you?

Woman Yes. Is that you?

Man Yes.

Woman Are we found?

Man We are. Are you all right, my dearest?

Woman I'm not bloody sure. Are you all right?

Man Yes. Would you care for a night stroll?

Woman Very well.

They put down the slippers and begin whistling as they walk to meet at the bed corner. She slips on her slippers then links with him. They set off pleasantly strolling.

This is a good way.

Man Yes.

Woman This corner's tricky.

Man (*agreeing*) Uh, uh.

They walk on.

Woman Are we on a sleepwalk?

Man No.

Woman Well, why aren't we in bed then?

Both (*remembering*) The glass of water!

Man It's here somewhere.

Woman There's not many places left.

They reach the drawers. They look at them. She opens bottom drawer. Searches one side.

Not in here.

He searches the other side.

Man No no.

Woman A vest. Whose is this vest?

Man (*as he moves on to next drawer*) We'll never know.

They search.

Not in here.

Woman She's depending on us.

As she passes to next drawer.

Man She is.

As he joins her at drawer.

Both We mustn't fail now.

They search.

Man Not here.

Both Where then?

Woman *looks up.* **Man** *follows the look. They see the cabinet high on the wall. They look at each other in acknowledgement.*

Man *begins to climb the drawers they have left out, as though they were a staircase.* **Woman** *holds his dressing-gown cord as he ascends. He climbs high until he reaches a level with the cabinet. He leans out and can just reach it. He manages to open it. And then things, things multitudinous come pouring, pouring out for a long, long time. It seems they will never stop. Then suddenly it is empty and we see just a glass left, but upside down on the shelf, empty, a thin light cutting through it, making it glint in its emptiness.* **Man** *reaches up for it and takes it out.*

Both Empty empty empty.

They begin to weep. This wakens **Spinster** *who gets up. She notices at the bed corner a bit of sheet sticks out; she crawls over to it, she tugs it, tugs it back, then peels it right back off the corner.*

*Underneath is soft black soil. She takes from under the bed a big
spade and digs into the earth, digs again. The sound wakes the
sleepers, who stand and step forward in a straight line facing the
audience.* **Spinster** *begins to rake through the soil with her hands.
She finds a small plaque on old wood. She passes it to* **Bosom
Lady** *who passes it to* **Charles** *who passes it to* **Marjorie** *who
passes it to* **Captain.** **Captain** *instantly breaks into tears at the
sight of it.* **Spinster** *rakes up more, finds a little baby's shoe. She
passes to* **Bosom Lady** *who passes to* **Charles** *who passes to*
Marjorie. **Marjorie** *bursts into tears.* **Spinster** *rakes on, she finds
a letter, she passes to* **Bosom Lady** *who passes to* **Charles** *who
bursts into tears. She finds a photograph. She passes to* **Bosom
Lady** *who immediately cries. She rakes more. She finds a little lace
handkerchief, she begins crying herself at this, and then into it. The
others gather around the patch of earth as though at a grave side
and slowly let their objects fall back into the earth, still weeping.*
Spinster *passes the handkerchief up to the others and they each dry
their tears with it as she again buries the past. The hanky reaches*
Bosom Lady *last, she dries her tears then sees* **The Couple**
*are crying too and passes it up to them. They cry into it. Spinster has
re-covered the earth and then, along with the others, returns to bed
and sleep.* **The Couple** *cry into the handkerchief. It is so wet* **Woman**
*wrings it out. It begins filling the glass. They are overjoyed. Happy,
they start laughing.*

Lights fade on them.

Lights up on **Bosom Lady** *who has caught the laughter and is
giggling in her sleep. She suddenly wakens and sits up laughing,
throwing from under the blankets, thousands of bras of all types
high into the air. They fall all over the bed.*

Bosom Lady How wonderful to just wake and bra around.

Suddenly **Sermon Head** *emerges from among the bras. One is
stuck over his face and he makes a muted complaint. She sees him,
removes the bra. . .*

Oh my Sermon.

*. . . and kisses him passionately all over his head and face, leaving
gigantic kiss marks. He is helpless in this to stop her, and screaming*

at top pitch. She covers his face with her bosom. We hear his muffled screaming. She takes her bosom away; he's still screaming. She puts it back over his face.

Awww dear, look in my medicine chest.

She takes it back. He is making a different sound now as though in shock, but still moaning. **Charles** *sits up, wraps a bra around* **Sermon Head**'s *face and fastens it at the back to shut him up.* **Bosom Lady** *starts kissing* **Charles**.

Charles Oh goodness gracious.

He disappears under the sheets. She turns out to the audience.

Bosom Lady In a way I am her Bosom majesty. Let me tell you, life has been just one long feather boa continually in the air! It has. If I look back along it I see one perfectly empty glass after another, and I can see in them the shimmering reflections of good food and cherries and chandeliers. I wouldn't know what 'stage' of life I am at now. But I do know when I exit through sleep, I make my entrance onto a little 'stage', lit through dusty bulbs and bedside lamps. Some nights there's a Berlin cabaret on, or a circus, a Can-Can, or my favourite, an English Music Hall, with a good all round bill of healthy entertainment.

Sermon Head *squeaks, squeaks, behind the bra. She looks round at him.*

The comedy duo!

She goes back to **Sermon Head** *and undoes bra. He is gasping in air.*
(*As a comedian.*) I say, I say, why don't you face up to it and go to the party.

Sermon Head *mouth open, shaking his head, lost.*

I s'pose it is difficult when you've no*body* to go with.

Cymbals crash.

Every one a winner, every one a gem.
Oh that crazy stage. Sand dancers, fan dancers, acrobats, then me. Doing my speciality act 'The juggling of many bras'

or giving a song, a belter, or the other kind, dedicated to some man of mine. I take up my stance, my big armpits are sucking in and ready for whoosh, my big fluttery hands opening. And then there's music on the air, everywhere, a melody under the mattress, stray notes all over the bed, then rising, calling out to have a song flown on them.

Sings the Rogers and Hart song 'Dancing On The Ceiling'.

After the first verse **Sermon Head** *joins her in singing the rest of the song, as they all go through a dance routine, based on sleep movements etc. while still lying in bed. It ends. They return to sleep.*

Blackout.

Pin light on **Sermon Head.**

Sermon Head Sermon Head in bed. I've made it. But really what a waste. Beaten, ravaged, yet still unrested. Even in such a bed as this, sleep can resist me. I give up. I give up everything. I give up even the trying. (*Depressed, silent.*) Wait something's happening. My eyes they're going. Jaw too. I'm slipping little inside. Look at me nodding. (*Head nods.*) Can, can this be sleep at long, long last. (*As he speaks this his head is lowering towards mattress.*)

Just as his cheek hits the delicious bed, **Captain** *lets out an enormous snore.* **Sermon Head** *springs back upright and awake.*

No.

Very angry now but no sound. He just bites into the sheets beside him, then spins upstage. This causes the sheets to be tugged slightly off the sleepers, disturbing them.

Marjorie *stands up in a sleepwalk way. The others stand too and link hands. As this is happening* **The Couple** *approach the bed with the glass of tears.* **Marjorie** *leads the others around the mattress to meet them. She stops, takes the drink, then carries on around the mattress and back to her place with everyone holding hands and following her in a long chain.* **The Couple** *catch on at the end and step back onto the bed.* **Marjorie** *picks up her pillow and crawls to sit on the extreme end of the bed holding it. The others gather up their pillows and scatter randomly all over the bed.*

They settle to sleep, clutching their pillows.

Marjorie Oh I. Well. Yes, yes.
We'd been married only a short time by then. He went in
the morning in the evening returned. Still clean. I had it
quiet and tidy for him. The clock ticking, he read the
newspaper up in front of his face, legs crossed, dark socks
on and long ankles. I'd sit and sometimes just look at his big
shoe hanging from the ankle. And he might lower the
newspaper and look over it at me staring, and I would start
as though waking from a dream and blush. And the blush
was always a cold blush, if you know what I mean. When I
served his dinner, the laying of the plate and the cutlery
always sounded out loud on the cloth, on our wedding table
under the window. I always had my hair up in a tight bun
then. And my style of clothes were the same, same as they
are now really, same as the house, as him, as his clothes and
socks. Which I wrung out through the wringer but these
were things that he never saw. He just saw the house as it
was when he left when he returned, Hello, pulling up his
trousers at the knee, sitting, the clock tick, the cloth, the
plate, the cutlery going down into the cloth, cruet, the pale
light coming through the netted curtains. The electric light
on in winter. He never really touched me, how can I say,
properly, once when my hair was slightly falling he pushed
it back up the neck, I felt two hard fingers there, they were
there for just a second too long, then gone. The personal
part of our life was like a jolt. I would taste his pyjamas in
my mouth from his shoulder. After he'd done with me he'd
lay back sweating a little, his eyes open then squeezed shut,
he didn't let the lids drop but squeezed them shut and slept
like that all night. It was maybe that night that it happened.
I told him quietly and he nodded quietly and said he was
pleased and it would be all right. And we telephoned his
sister in Bournemouth and both told her over the phone,
and she kept saying 'How loverly, well you two, well'. But
after that it was hardly mentioned. The front door would
go. The plate would go on the table. I'd see some dust on
the radio top and think how did I miss it. He'd step in and
the newspaper and the same. But it was all right because
within all this our baby was growing. Warm inside, glowing,

and it passed up to my face and my new chubby cheeks. (*She
pinches them.*) When I started it was before he went to work
luckily. And he ran me to the town hospital, took me in, left
for work. I remember seeing his dark head pass the one two
three windows. While I stood in my coat waiting to be seen
by Sister, a nice woman, but such cracked hands. And as
soon as she touched me I knew something was wrong inside,
it felt cold, dead, hollow as though a draught was getting in
and all I could think of was his boiled ham on the plate
before the vegetables were placed round it and the clean
white fat on the edge and his yellow mustard across the
colours, horrible yellow, almost green and the meat too
pink, unnatural, and unnatural, an unnatural shape. And
the baby was dead when she came out, she was gone when
she came out. And when he was told he nodded and when
he was told he nodded. And later at home I did this (*A
gesture, like holding a baby*) and later at home I did this and
after that there were no more jolts in the night and after
that we spoke even less and we stayed that way. And I
didn't BLOODY CARE LOVE! And though it was winter
and though I was still weak I went out into the garden in the
snow and I threw my wish away.

*Soft white feathers begin to fall in a shower. The others awaken.
They lift their faces to it.* **Sermon Head** *revolves to face front.*
Captain *flicks snow off* **Marjorie**'s *hair and shoulders. The feather
fall is very heavy now.* **Charles** *puts up a big brolly; they all come
underneath it. The snow feathers falling. All of them, except*
Sermon Head, *sing a lullaby ('Loo la bye bye'). It finishes.*
Charles *slowly brings the brolly forward and down so that it covers
them all from view. On it is written —*

GOOD NIGHT

Further titles in the Methuen Modern Plays series are listed overleaf.

	Mr Puntila and His Man Matti
	The Resistible Rise of Arturo Ui
	A Respectable Wedding & Other One-Act
	Plays
	The Rise and Fall of the City of Mahagonny
	& Seven Deadly Sins
	St Joan of the Stockyards
	Schweyk in the Second World War &
	The Visions of Simone Machard
	The Threepenny Opera
Brecht ⎫	
Weill ⎬	*Happy End*
Lane ⎭	
Howard Brenton	*Bloody Poetry*
	The Churchill Play
	Epsom Downs
	Plays for the Poor Theatre
	Revenge
	The Romans in Britain
Howard Brenton	*Brassneck*
David Hare	*Pravda*
Mikhail Bulgakov	*The White Guard*
Jim Cartwright	*Bed*
	Road
	To
Caryl Churchill	*Serious Money*
	Softcops & Fen
	Top Girls
Noël Coward	*Hay Fever*
Sarah Daniels	*Masterpieces*
Shelagh Delaney	*A Taste of Honey*
David Edgar	*Destiny*
	Entertaining Strangers
	Teendreams & Our Own People
	That Summer
Dario Fo	*Accidental Death of an Anarchist*
	Archangels Don't Play Pinball
	Can't Pay? Won't Pay!
	Elizabeth